MW00784424

THIS SKETCHBOOK BELONGS TO ....

CONTACT ....